What is a
Christian?

Roger's enthusiasm for Jesus is infectious and, through his ministry, many have caught the bug! This little book bubbles over with life as we're pointed again and again to the Lord Jesus. A great introduction for enquirers.

Glen Scrivener
Evangelist, Revival Media, Eastbourne

Roger writes to feed and challenge the intellect, to warm the heart and to pull at the will for a clear response. This is not only a book; it is a compelling and convincing evangelistic talk! There is huge confusion as people answer this question and this book helpfully deals with all the reason for that confusion. There is a real honesty about the bad news for people, but a wonderful joy about the good news. It is all written by a man who's heart has so obviously been gripped by the Lord Jesus and His wonderful gospel.

Tim Hanson
Vicar, Christ Church Wharton, Winsford

Reading a Carswell book in my teens kept me following Jesus, so I'm always interested in the latest offering from Roger's pen. *What is a Christian* is a clear, compelling and concise introduction to the life of faith. It's amazing how much wonderful truth can be squeezed into just 80 pages!

Dave Gobbett
Associate Pastor, Eden Baptist Church, Cambridge

What is a Christian?

Roger Carswell

CHRISTIAN FOCUS

Roger Carswell was as a secondary school teacher in West Yorkshire. For over thirty years he has worked full-time speaking around the world to students and adults about the believability of the Christian faith and its relevance to modern life. He is married to Dot and they have four children.

Unless otherwise indicated scripture quotations taken from the *Holy Bible, New International Version*. Copyright © 1973, 1978, 1984 by International Bible Society. Used by permission of Hodder & Stoughton Publishers, A member of the Hodder Headline Group. All rights reserved. 'NIV' is a registered trademark of International Bible Society. UK trademark number 1448790.

Scripture quotations marked 'NKJV' are taken from the *New King James Version*. Copyright © 1982 by Thomas Nelson, Inc. Used by permission. All rights reserved.

Scripture quotations marked 'NASB' are taken from the *New American Standard Bible®*, Copyright © 1960, 1962, 1963, 1968, 1971, 1972, 1973, 1975, 1977, 1995 by The Lockman Foundation Used by Permission. (www.Lockman.org)

Scripture quotations marked 'KJV' are taken from the *King James Version*. All rights reserved.

paperback ISBN 978-1-78191-272-0
epub ISBN 978-1-78191-282-9
Mobi ISBN 978-1-78191-283-6

© Roger Carswell

10 9 8 7 6 5 4 3 2 1

Published in 2013
by
Christian Focus Publications, Ltd.,
Geanies House, Fearn, Ross-shire,
IV20 1TW, Great Britain.
www.christianfocus.com

Cover design by Daniel van Straaten

Printed by 🖨 Grafica Veneta

Contents

Acknowledgements

I am grateful to Peter and Pim Claridge of Crow-borough, Janice Bowman of Leicestershire and Emma Balch of Hay-on-Wye, whose comments, improvements and corrections have not only put icing on the cake but enhanced the ingredients of this little book.

Thanks to you too, for obtaining, and I hope reading, this book.

Dedication

To my faithful and caring friends

Chris Marsden, Frank Brearley, David Gibb, Matt Mattai and Malcolm and Christine Watts

who for many years have been my Advisory Board, protecting me from myself, guiding me in my decisions and encouraging me in my ministry as a Christian. Thank you!

Introduction

The title of this book should, according to good grammar, be, '*Who* exactly is a Christian?' but that tilts the book away from what it is about. This little volume is unpacking the distinctives that make Christian belief so vibrant and joyful. It attempts to unearth the core beliefs that real Christians have in common. All true Christians have a basic structure in their faith that unites them to other believers.

In 1962 the American and British scientists James Watson and Francis Crick won the Nobel Prize in Medicine for their work. They are widely recognised as being pioneers in the work of discovering DNA. It was one of the most significant scientific discoveries of the 20th century. DNA is the material in humans and almost all other organisms, which makes us what we are. It stores and encodes the information which forms the building blocks of life.

This little book examines the 'DNA' of Christians. Despite all Christians possessing different physical features, personalities, and cultural backgrounds, as well as varying peripheral concerns, there are core beliefs which are basic to those who have truly put their trust in Jesus. Of course, we know that many, especially in the West, claim the name 'Christian' but are not following Jesus. For them, it is social and cultural. But what is it that people who are more than nominal Christians believe? What are the building blocks of real Christian faith? What is basic for the person who has come to know God in a dynamic and intimate relationship? What is the Christian's DNA?

I hope that you will enjoy reading. It may not help you to win the Nobel Prize, but I pray that it will introduce you to the true and living God who is, after all, the Author of DNA!

One

What does it matter anyway?

At a circus an elephant was tethered to an eighteen-inch stake. The huge beast could easily have pulled it out of the ground and become free, but he didn't even try. The circus owners had tied him to the same post since he was a baby. He had tried repeatedly to break free, but found that he couldn't and so concluded that he could never pull the stake out of the ground. So there he stood, a massive creature capable of lifting whole trees, yet held captive by a puny piece of wood.

In a similar way, throughout our early years we can all too easily pick up negative ideas of who Jesus is, and what He did. For some, on both the outside and inside of the church, it looks messy and complicated, and others have had bad experiences of church. Christian belief and church can be portrayed and perceived as appealing only to the weak-minded and easily deceived, appearing irrelevant and/or untrue. So it is a serious challenge to break away from that which tethers a person's mind, to take a closer look at the Christian message, to break free from a mindset formed in childhood and seek to be objective about Jesus.

A God-shaped hole?

And yet, something within us gives us a sense of awareness of there being more to this life than 'threescore years and ten'. When we stand at the graveside of a loved one, or see a stunning sunset, or feel the intensity of the joy of life, we resound to the truth of the Bible's words that 'God has put eternity in the human heart'. There is too much around us to believe that the only dimension is materialist. We are naturally curious and wonder why we are here and what life is really about.

The late Helen Keller, whose sight and hearing were destroyed by an illness before she was two years of age, expressed this awareness of God when just a teenager. She was to become a truly inspirational woman. Anne Sullivan who lived with Keller and taught her for many years thought it would be impossible to teach little Helen about God. But when Helen was fourteen, Miss Sullivan placed her sensitive fingers on her lips and slowly spelled out 'G-O-D.' It was a breakthrough.

Helen's face lit up and she exclaimed, 'Oh, I am so glad you told me His name, for He has often spoken to me.'

Even in today's secular age, there is a steady stream of people who want to break free from cynical unbelief, which has held them captive for so long.

Melvyn Bragg, author and broadcaster - and certainly not a convinced Christian – describing his 'first steps back on the road to faith' wrote, 'Stephen Hawking speaks of worlds of thought which we shall never know – there is the inexplicable. I think most of us sense that now and then we have pulses from it – in passion, in daydreams, "surprised by joy" … the current notion that atheistic reason marks the high point of human intelligence, strikes me as very doubtful. I'm as certain as can be that there's more to come.'[1]

Human beings are essentially religious. The hearts of men and women are instinctively aware of God. It was the way we were created to be. That is why something grates when one listens to atheists. We know they haven't got the answers. We find people worshipping on the banks of the Ganges; praying with their faces turned toward the sun, the moon, the East, or Mecca, in a temple, a chapel or cathedral or communing privately with their Heavenly Father. Humans are essentially devout. Alain de Botton, author of 'Religion for atheists', helped set up 'The School of Life', which runs a course called, 'How to fill the God-shaped hole'. We were created with a spiritual dimension; we were made to know God, and He just cannot be shaken off. The One who brought all things into being has you and me as part of His design. We pursue God because He has put an urge within us that spurs us to do so.

Christianity is still making an impact

The claims of Christianity and its impact are such that it is totally unwise to ignore them. We do so at our peril. We are repeatedly told by some that all religions are more or less the same. Yet even the most casual look at Christianity demonstrates how far that is from the truth. Only in Christianity is there belief in one God who is Father, Son and Holy Spirit; only in Christianity do people rely on what God has done to save them, rather than hoping that their own efforts are sufficient to save them; only in Christianity is there a Saviour who not only died for them, but rose again from the dead. And only in Christianity is there the Holy Spirit who guides, encourages and supports those who trust in God. That is why Christians say they actually *know* God in a personal way. That is why it is only Christians who have a certainty about life after death because they are depending on what God has done for them, rather than what they do for Him.

Of course, Christians make mistakes and get things wrong. There ought never to be smugness in Christianity. Our only claim is that whilst we have messed up, God has come to our rescue. We are what we are because of what He has done for us. Nevertheless we have been changed, and the results of that are very noticeable even by those who are opposed to Christian belief.

Atheistic journalist Matthew Parris, writing of his experience of growing up in Nyasaland (today called Malawi), reflected, '... travelling in Malawi refreshed another belief, too: one I've been trying to banish all my life, but an observation I've been unable to avoid since my African childhood. It confounds my ideological beliefs, stubbornly refuses to fit my world view, and has embarrassed my growing belief that there is no God ... I've become convinced of the enormous contribution that Christian evangelism makes in Africa ... Christianity changes people's hearts. It brings spiritual transformation. The rebirth is real. The change is good ... far from having cowed or confined its converts, their faith appeared to have liberated and relaxed them.'[2]

Roy Hattersley, politician and journalist, wrote in the *Guardian*, under the strap-line, 'We atheists have to accept that most believers are better human beings'. He said that repeatedly he felt his own atheism was being challenged by Christians he saw. Here is a typical comment:

Last week a middle-ranking officer of the Salvation Army, who gave up a well-paid job to devote his life to the poor, attempted to convince me that homosexuality is a sin. Late at night, on the streets of one of our great cities, that man offers friendship as well as help to the most degraded and degenerate human beings … and he does what he believes to be his Christian duty without the slightest suggestion of disapproval. Yet, for much of his time, he is meeting needs that result from conduct he regards as intrinsically wicked.[3]

And again Alain de Botton, a non-believer, argues that agnostics and atheists should steal from religion and gain from them insights into building a sense of community, making our relationships last, overcoming feelings of envy and inadequacy, escaping the twenty-four hour media, and creating new businesses designed to address our emotional needs! He has even devised Ten Commandments for atheists. But he has no answer to the problems of sin, guilt or death, and no one to give the desire or power to live according to the standards he has devised.

Jesus defines Christianity

The central Christian belief is that through Jesus' death on a cross twenty centuries ago, we can have forgiveness and be given a new start. For Christians, the one subject which defines them is not a creed but a Person. It is all about Jesus. He is the One who was anticipated through the ages prior to His birth. In fact the Old Testament, written long before Jesus was born, prophesies about Him in such detail that we are told where He would be born – in a tiny village called Bethlehem, eight miles from Jerusalem; how He would be born of a virgin;

details of His life, teaching and works; and about His crucifixion in minute detail, even though crucifixion was not devised as a means of execution till many centuries later. Prophecies of old, repeated by Jesus throughout His life, made it clear that He would die for the sins of the world, be buried and three days later rise from the dead.

The Christian is clear that Jesus is the Lord to whom they have submitted and before whom one day every human will bow. He is the Saviour they trust to rescue them from their plight of sin and rebellion. He, through the Holy Spirit, is their Companion, whom they rely on to guide and guard them through life's journey. He is the King, the rightful ruler, whose government is legitimate and perfect and will one day be manifest across the world. He is the Judge before whom every individual will give account. He is the One they love, follow and seek to be like because He first loved them and gave Himself for them.

The One God is Father, Son and Holy Spirit. There was love and relationship manifested between each Person in the Trinity throughout the aeons of eternity past. But it was always God's plan that in 'the fullness of time' the Son would step into the arena of human history, manifest in a human body. He was the God-Man. Centuries earlier God had told Moses that he and his people should call God, 'I am'. Jesus took on Himself this very name that God's people used when speaking of Him. So repeatedly Jesus called Himself 'I am'. His hearers knew exactly what He was saying, and some even attempted to stone Him to death because they felt He was blaspheming.

Jesus' miracles were a demonstration of His power, signs that He was who He claimed to be: miraculously He fed the hungry, cured the blind, the deaf, the mute, the paralysed, the lame and the leprous. He calmed the storm at sea, raised the dead, and turned water into wine. He lived a pure, spotless life that could not be faulted. And yet He knew what it was to be hungry, tired, tempted and thirsty. He felt pain, sorrow and isolation.

Jesus came for sinners

Christians, though, are incredibly grateful that, as Jesus expressed it, He came into the world to save sinners. Every Christian wants to respond to that, saying, 'I qualify!' Jesus did not come into the world for good people – He would never have found any. Outside of God Himself, who truly is good? Throughout His life, Jesus was meeting with and transforming people whose lives had been wrecked by their wrong choices and sinful deeds.

The woman of Samaria had had five husbands and was now living with another man when she met Jesus. She was never to be the same again, as she found Jesus to be source of 'living water that would never run dry' who completely changed and satisfied her, giving her life meaning again.

Zacchaeus was a tax collector for the Roman occupiers, known for being corrupt and exploitative so he could line his own pockets. He was not even permitted to worship in the synagogue because he was regarded as a traitor. Yet when Jesus was nearing his home town of Jericho, Zacchaeus climbed a sycamore tree to get a good look at the One about whom everyone was speaking. Jesus saw him, called him down, went to his house to talk and dine, which was to change his life – he promised to give half of all his possessions to the poor, and return four-fold what he had taken from the people.

A woman caught in the actual act of committing adultery, was dragged by the hypocritical religious leaders to Jesus. She was literally a stone's throw away from death, as they wanted her executed. Jesus challenged them with the words, 'If any one of you is without sin, let him be the first to throw the first stone at her.' Jesus was the only person there without sin, but He did not want to put her to death. Slowly her accusers all sloped off leaving only Jesus and the woman. He did not condemn her but gave her the command, the desire and the power to 'go now and leave your life of sin.'[4]

Jesus could do this because He was determined to go to Jerusalem where He would be crucified, and carry upon Himself the sin of the world. He would die, be buried, and then rise from the dead. His works throughout His life were amazing, but there is a sense in which Jesus came to do three days' work, which were the times of greatest suffering as He bore the pain and the penalty of sin and death on our behalf, then rose triumphantly from the dead.

For two thousand years men and women from all countries, classes and cultures have found Christ to be not only their Lord and Saviour but their Helper and Friend. He means so much to them that they want everyone to know Him in the way that they have experienced Him. They have found that they have been loved by God, not for what they are, but for what Jesus has done for them, and their life is bound up in His.

Christianity is not a set of dogmas upon which we are to sign on the dotted line. It is about entering into a relationship with the living God in a life-transforming way. To know God is to have the Maker of all things, living by His Holy Spirit within one's life; it is to be made a child of God, and to be secure in His keeping through life, death and throughout eternity. The person who knows God reverences Him. He is, after all, God!

Jesus is still relevant today

But the question remains as to whether this is still important today. Is religion in the genes of some but not others? Are some simply more religiously inclined than others? Inevitably upbringing is important, but there is within every person a nature which was created to know

God. Around us there are thousands of pointers to the Maker of all things. There is, too, the possibility of a life lived with God Himself as the constant companion who keeps closer than anyone else could, to lead and protect the person who trusts Him.

God promises that He will be with them even as they go through death. Whilst apprehensive about the process of death, the Christian is uniquely unafraid of death itself, knowing that being 'absent from the body is to be present with the Lord'. In fact, like autumn leaves, the true Christian character is often seen in its greatest beauty just prior to death. But above and beyond this is the fact that there is coming a day when every individual will stand before God in judgement. He will pronounce each individual's eternal destiny. The Bible knows nothing of Dante or Milton who embellish the thought of doom, but rather leaves eternity itself to fill in the details. This is how the apostle John describes judgement in the last book of the Bible:

> Then I saw a great white throne and him who was seated on it. Earth and sky fled from his presence, and there was no place for them. And I saw the dead, great and small, standing before the throne, and books were opened. Another book was opened, which is the book of life. The dead were judged according to what they had done as recorded in the books. The sea gave up the dead that were in it, and Death and Hades gave up the dead that were in them, and each person was judged according to

what he had done. Then Death and Hades were thrown into the lake of fire. The lake of fire is the second death. If anyone's name was not found written in the book of life, he was thrown into the lake of fire.[5]

There is a blinding purity and holiness to the Imperial Throne of God. This is a judgement which cannot be avoided. The Bible teaches that nations, cities, rulers, churches, angels and people will all be judged. According to Greek legend, in the 4th century B.C. Damocles spoke out of turn to the king of Syracuse in Sicily at a royal banquet. He was condemned to sit under a sword suspended by a single human hair. There is a sense in which every one of us sits under a 'Sword of Damocles' if we have not made sure that all is well between us and God.

God will judge us all

In the Bible, it is clear that a day is fixed for this great day of judgement, for God 'has set a day when He will judge the world with justice by the Man He has appointed. He has given proof of this to all men by raising Him from the dead.'[6] The scene in the Bible passage above, is frightening, but there is benefit for even the atheist, for it is a moment of truth after years of denying God. The creature will face the Creator. The accused are all God's foes. Judgement for those whose sin has been forgiven, who are 'in Christ', has already taken place at the cross where Jesus died. The judgement here is reserved for those who have said 'no' to Him. The judgement will be fair because God is too wise to be mistaken and too kind to be unjust. Judgement will not be according to our enemies who might hate us, or our friends who love us, but according to truth.

Many people rely on their good deeds to save them, but the problem with relying on our works is that we are all nevertheless guilty of sins, which would condemn us. There needs to be forgiveness now to guarantee that all will be well when we meet God in eternity. The sentence He pronounces will be final. Perhaps the worst aspect of hell is the word, 'forever'. And any appeal is futile, in that there will be no questioning the fairness of the judgement, which is made by the all-knowing God. Yet, He who will decide our eternal destiny is the One who has loved us so much that He came to earth with the express mission of going to the cross to die paying the penalty for sin.

I love the story I once heard the American evangelist Billy Graham tell. Apparently, he was stopped by a police sheriff for speeding. As the policeman began speaking with the evangelist, he suddenly realised who he was, and then told Billy Graham that he had been converted to Christ whilst listening to him preach. They chatted for a few minutes, when the sheriff asked again, 'But anyway, do you know what speed you were doing?' Billy Graham admitted that he did, and had to go with the sheriff to the police station. There he was given an on-the-spot fine. As Billy Graham went to his pocket for his cheque book, the sheriff interjected, 'Oh no,' he said, 'I'll pay this one!' The sheriff actually paid the penalty he had imposed on the guilty man. In a much bigger way, that is what Jesus has done for us. We are guilty, but out of His great love He has died, the righteous for the unrighteous, paying for our sin and guilt. To neglect or reject that is to refuse God's way of reconciliation and forgiveness.

There is nothing more important than considering Jesus – who He is, what He has done, and what the gospel, or Good News, is all about. What we believe about God is the most important thing about us. But first we need to see what we can actually know about Him.

ENDNOTES

1   *Daily Telegraph*, Saturday, 11 June 2011
2   *The Times*, Saturday, December 27, 2008
3   *The Guardian*, Monday, September 12, 2005
4   John 8:7 &11
5   Revelation 20:11-15
6   See Acts 17:31

Two

A Christian has recognised who God is

Increasingly, large sections of the media are portraying God as the mythical figure conjured up in the minds of the intellectually or emotionally weak. Atheists have been given disproportionate chunks of influence and time on television and in education. And of course, this has made an impact on the thinking of the masses. Television has become the opiate of the people. That is dangerous because it leaves us open to manipulation.

Strangely though, people who are marked by their unbelief cannot erase God from their thinking. It seems that they must speak against Him and His followers, unable to eliminate God from their minds. If I may

illustrate with a far less significant issue, I do not believe
in Santa Claus, but I don't see it as my purpose in life to
take hold of the under-sixes who do and put them right.
So what is it about God that He is in the minds of not
only His followers, but of those who deny Him?

Others may not feel confident in their non-belief, but
are nevertheless questioning about the God of the Bible.
C.S.Lewis, famed author and professor of Medieval and
Renaissance English at Cambridge University, wrote,
'The ancient man approached God (or even the gods)
as the accused person approaches his judge. For the
modern man the roles are reversed. He is the judge:
God is in the dock. He is quite a kindly judge: if God
should have a reasonable defence for being the god who
permits war, poverty and disease, he is ready to listen to
it. The trial may even end in God's acquittal. But the
important thing is that Man is on the bench and God
in the dock.'[1]

Then there are millions of devoutly religious people
throughout the world, who sincerely worship a god or
gods who is/are far from the Being whom Christians
claim to know in a personal way.

Did we create God?
Is it a question of simply tossing a coin and choosing
a religion depending on your place of origin? Is it
possible to have any certainty about whether there
is a God, who is, by definition, invisible, intangible,
supernatural? And if so, to know what God is like?

To try to imagine God is to create an imaginary god. But central to Christian belief is that the true, eternal God has revealed Himself to humanity. What we know about God is what He has told us. Evidence of His existence is seen in creation all around us. There is every indication that there is design, purpose and order which each points towards a Designer, a Creator. Whatever the possibility of all that we know coming about through the coincidence of accidents over billions of years, there can still never have been nothing. Something does not come from nothing! Something cannot come from nothing. God always has been; He is eternal.

It is settled in the wisdom of the ages that there can never have been nothing, because something does not come from nothing. In the 1st century Rabbi Akiba Ben Joseph said, 'A house testifies that there was a builder, a dress that there was a weaver, a door that there was a carpenter; so our world by its existence proclaims its Creator, God.' Nothing in modern science or philosophy has been able to disprove such straightforward logic. The world must have had an origin, which must have had a cause. That cause must have been intelligent and powerful, and He has revealed Himself as God. I think the author of *Gulliver's Travels*, Jonathan Swift (1667–1745), summarised this point when he said, 'That the universe was formed by a fortuitous concourse of atoms, I will no more believe than that the accidental jumbling of the alphabet would fall into a most ingenious treatise of philosophy.'

There has yet to be an explanation of what went 'bang' in the theory of the big bang, or of how life came from non-life? Just as Robinson Crusoe was aware of Man Friday because of the footprints in the sand, so we are pointed towards the existence of God in the wonder of creation. God may be ignored but He can never be evaded. The marks of His presence are everywhere.

The vastness of creation is overwhelming, beyond anything our finite minds can grasp. The distances in space are so great that we can only use the speed of light (186,000 miles per second) travelling *for one whole year* (a light year, about 5,879,000,000,000 miles) to measure them!

Robert Jastrow, a former head of NASA's Goddard Center, wrote the following to help us grasp the immensity of the universe:

> An analogy will help to clarify the meaning of these enormous distances. Let the sun be the size of an orange; on that scale of sizes the earth is a grain of sand circling in orbit around the sun at a distance of 10 metres; the giant planet Jupiter, 11 times larger than the earth, is a cherry pip revolving at a distance of about 100 metres; Saturn is another cherry pip 200 metres from the sun; and Pluto, the outermost planet, is still another sand grain at a distance of 1,000 metres from the sun.

> On the same scale the average distance between the stars is 2000 miles. The sun's nearest neighbour, a star called

Alpha Centauri, is 1300 miles away. In the space between the sun and its neighbours there is nothing but a thin distribution of hydrogen atoms, forming a vacuum far better than any ever achieved on earth. The galaxy, on this scale, is a cluster of oranges separated by an average distance of 2000 miles, the entire cluster being 20 million miles in diameter.

An orange, a few grains of sand some feet away, and then some cherry pips circling slowly around the orange at a distance of a 100 metres. Two thousand miles away is another orange, perhaps with a few specks of planetary matter circling around it.[2]

What is God like?

Belief in God does not mean that we have understood everything concerning what God is like. Through the Bible - God's written word - and through Jesus – God's living Word – God has made known to us exactly who He is.[3]

God is self-sufficient. He exists in His own right. He does not need anything that He has made, and yet He loves His creation. As the infinite God, He is able to love each individual with infinite capacity. When Jesus died for the world, He died for us individually, just as much as if we – you and I – were the only ones in the world.

C.S. Lewis said that God is so 'brim-full of existence' that He can give existence away, can cause things to be, and to be really other than Himself.

Our beliefs about God are not a result of random guesswork from religious leaders of the past. Rather, they rest on what God has revealed about Himself in the Bible and through Jesus. That does not mean that we finite creatures can fathom all the depths of the mind of the infinite God. If I could understand all there is to know about God, either He would not be God, or I would not be a mere man. A comprehended god is no God at all. But just because He is beyond comprehension, does not mean that He does not exist. If His mind - which we see in His word and works - is so vast, what must His mind be in all its fullness and infinity? His ways are higher than our ways, but He has made Himself known to us.

God is a Trinity

The Bible underlines the fact that there is one God, who is Father, Son and Holy Spirit. The three Persons of the Godhead act in harmonious unity in all the mighty works throughout the universe. In every great work of God throughout the Bible each Person of the Trinity is at work, whether it be in creation, in the incarnation (the birth of Jesus), His baptism, His death on the cross for us, His resurrection from the dead, or even the bringing of an individual to faith in Him. Christians believe that there are three witnesses in heaven: the Father, the Word – Jesus, and the Holy Spirit; and these three are one. God does not exist in isolation or solitude but in three persons, in one essence. He is infinite in His unity. The Bible says, 'The Lord, He is God; there is none else beside Him.'[4] Within the Godhead there is relationship and love.

God is spirit. He cannot be placed in a scientific laboratory and examined. Those who know Him do so in spirit and in truth. He is all-powerful, meaning that He can do all things; some are immense while others appear minute, but He is in control. As He works He does not tire or become weary. We cannot measure God's power by our strength, for His is infinite. He is the One who controls every atom, every planet. He guides the millions of stars, the great constellations and unnumbered universes. Nothing is impossible with God.

God knows everything

I used to be troubled over the idea that God knows all things – including my heart and mind - wondering how this could be possible. The advent of Google has made God's omniscience seem straightforward to me! We humans have spent millions of hours trying to discover the things that God brought into being by just a word. He knows our yesterdays, todays and tomorrows. God is never taken by surprise. There is never an emergency Cabinet Meeting in heaven where God is wondering what to do! He has never said, 'I didn't expect that!' He knows the hearts of us all. His knowledge and wisdom are not learned from others.

God is everywhere

'We may ignore, but we can nowhere evade the presence of God. The world is crowded with Him. He walks everywhere incognito,' said C.S.Lewis. The Bible insists that God is omnipresent. God does not ring the doorbell before He makes His presence felt. He is inescapable. If He were not a God of infinite love, this would be creepy, but for those who know God, it is a greatly comforting truth. 3,000 years ago King David wrote,

> Where can I go from your Spirit?
>> Where can I flee from your presence?
> If I go up to the heavens, you are there;
>> if I make my bed in the depths, you are there.
> If I rise on the wings of the dawn,
>> if I settle on the far side of the sea,
> even there your hand will guide me,
>> your right hand will hold me fast.
> If I say, 'Surely the darkness will hide me
>> and the light become night around me,'
> even the darkness will not be dark to you;
>> the night will shine like the day,
>> for darkness is as light to you.
> For you created my inmost being;
>> you knit me together in my mother's womb.
> I praise you because I am fearfully and wonderfully made;
>> your works are wonderful,
>> I know that full well.

My frame was not hidden from you
>   when I was made in the secret place.
When I was woven together in the depths of the earth,
>   your eyes saw my unformed body.
All the days ordained for me
>   were written in your book
>   before one of them came to be.
How precious to me are your thoughts, O God!
>   How vast is the sum of them!
Were I to count them,
>   they would outnumber the grains of sand.
When I awake,
>   I am still with you.[5]

When on Mars Hill in Athens, the apostle Paul presented the Christian message to a group of sceptical philoso-
phers who felt that God was unknown and unknowable.
He said, 'The God who made the world and everything
in it is the Lord of heaven and earth and does not live in
temples built by hands … He is not far from each one
of us. "For in Him we live and move and have our being."'[6] Of course, we may defy the purpose of God and
insulate ourselves from Him, but the fact remains that
He is there all the time.

God is everlasting
Earthly power goes from one leader to another, but
God is not like that. From everlasting to everlasting He

is God. He is before the beginning and beyond the end. God does not change. He is never in a bad mood. He is reliable and consistent. All His promises, of which there are thousands in the Bible, are reliable and trustworthy. God can never deny His own character, so He cannot sin and cannot lie. He *is* truth, and cannot be anything else.

God is holy
The Bible reveals that God is holy by nature. That doesn't simply mean that He has never sinned, though that is true, but that there is an intrinsic purity and unapproachable holiness in the character of God. He is light; there is no inner darkness in Him. This is an intense, blazing holiness which sees sin as abhorrent and sets God apart from everything else in His creation. It would be a frightening thought if we were to meet Him as we are. But if our sin has been forgiven, and we are covered in the righteousness of Jesus, then we will be accepted and embraced by Him.

God is just
Created, as we are, in God's image, people, and therefore, societies long for justice. There is something terrible when people feel they have been let down by the judiciary or treated unjustly. God is a just God. He is infinitely merciful, but He is just. He cannot be corrupted by even the most powerful of authorities. A holy God will display anger against sin. He is not

a weak deity who can be cajoled or enticed with pleading words. God sees everything. How can God who sees the tears of abused children, who witnesses the wholesale destruction of unborn babies across the globe, making the womb the least safe place to be, who observes greed, violence, spite, bitterness, drunkenness, immorality, blasphemy, selfishness and exploitation, not be angry? It is a foolish thing to pit popular 'wisdom' – that God is too kind to punish the ungodly – against the clear teaching of the Bible. We read in it that 'the wages of sin is death'. Jesus warned about a place of eternal punishment, of darkness where there would be weeping and gnashing of teeth, of unquenchable fire and torment, where people will be shut out from the presence of the Lord and the majesty of His power. Our world is fractured and in a state of rebellion against its Maker. We are guilty of calling evil good, and good evil. God's justice will prevail. And yet, alongside the theme of God's justice in the Bible, we read of God's love.[7]

God is perfect

God's character, as portrayed in the Bible, is the most perfect and beautiful conceivable. The words 'God is good' and 'God is love' are the most revolutionary in the world. Millions live their lives in fear that God may not be good. He is consistently good, totally reliable, and even when times are bad, God is good. There is an old song which Christians sometimes sing:

His love has no limit, His grace has no measure,
His power has no boundary known unto men
For out of His infinite riches in Jesus
He giveth, and giveth, and giveth again![8]

The greatest demonstration of the goodness and love of God is seen in the death of Jesus. At Calvary, the place where Jesus died, the wrath of God against sin, and the love of God for sinners met, as Jesus took on Himself the weight of the world's wrong. Out of love Jesus, who is Himself God, paid the penalty it would take us eternity to pay. This was God reaching down to rescue lost humanity, and reconciling us to Himself.

Nicolaus Copernicus, the Polish astronomer and scientist, was born in Torun in Poland in 1473. He was the founder of modern-day astronomy, and first came up with the notion that the earth rotates around the sun, rather than the other way round. A brilliant scholar, his picture hangs in St. John's Church in Torun. Beneath it is his epitaph and confession of faith: 'I do not ask the grace which Thou didst give Saint Paul; nor can I dare ask the grace which Thou didst grant to Saint Peter; but, the mercy which Thou didst show to the dying robber; that mercy show to me.' Because of the cross of Jesus, such mercy is promised to everyone who calls on the Name of the Lord.

ENDNOTES

1   C. S. Lewis, *God in the Dock*, Fount Publishing, 1998
2   Taken from, and then Anglicised, *Good News Magazine*, July – August, 2006
3   Why I believe the Bible to be God's Word, and Jesus to be God Himself, I have dealt with in the book, *Why believe?* published by Authentic Media.
4   Deuteronomy 4:35, KJV
5   Psalm 139:7-18
6   Acts 17:24 & 27-28
7   For a fuller examination of human suffering in a world made by a loving God, please see either *Where is God in a messed up world?* by Roger Carswell, IVP, or *Why doesn't God stop the trouble?* by Roger Carswell, CFP and 10Publishing.
8   Written by Annie Johnson Flint

Three

A Christian has repented of all that is wrong

Politician Chris Bryant and historian David Starkey are both vocal atheists. They are frequent panellists on the BBC's 'Question Time' programme. Some time ago they appeared together. In the course of the discussion, Chris Bryant said, 'There is no such thing as evil.' David Starkey, stunned by such an obviously false statement, responded saying, 'When the two planes flew into the twin towers on 11th September, 2001, that was evil!' It was the end of that little argument.

Many of us in the developed world enjoy life and want to hang on to it. With Louis Armstrong, we 'think to ourselves, what a wonderful world.' We appreciate friendship, family, love, kindness, wonder, beauty, and we are thankful for good food and drink, for laughter and medicine. But we know that is not the whole story.

The problem of Evil

At times, all of us shudder at the horror of some new atrocity. We have become accustomed to - but not immune to - the horror of war, terrorism, genocides, abuse, rape and murder. It is one of the awful aspects of growing from childhood to adolescence, that one is awakened to the realities of a world which is not at ease with itself. Headlines leave us cynical and suspicious, scarred by exposure to what is happening all around us. All too easily we blame politicians and rulers, who clearly are not altogether innocent. But neither are they wholly responsible for the world's ills.

Sections of the Bible are devoted to the messages of prophets, sent by God to confront the sins of nations, cities, rulers and people. Clearly, there is no novelty in acts of wickedness. And so often the 'innocent' suffer. James, the half-brother of Jesus, put his finger on the problem. He acknowledged the joy of living: 'Every good and perfect gift is from above, coming down from the Father of the heavenly lights, who does not change like shifting shadows,' but later writes, 'What causes fights and quarrels among you? Don't they come from your desires that battle within you? You want something but don't get it. You kill and covet, but you cannot have what you want.'[1] James is saying that the macro-problems of the world are a reflection of the micro-problems of individuals. A Christian is someone who has ceased pointing the finger at others. God never forgives an excuse. We need to recognise that the heart of the human problem is the problem of the human heart. God, in the person of Jesus, and in the written word, the Bible, refuses to flatter us, but exposes us for what we are. And our consciences usually concur with God's up-front diagnosis.

God's law is an expression of who He is. He has given to us His commandments, which not only show us what is right, but make it clear that we are wrong! They show us what we are really like. Jesus summarised the commandments by saying, 'You shall love the Lord your God with all your heart, with all your soul and with all your mind .... And you shall love your neighbour as yourself.'[2]

In His famous Sermon on the Mount, Jesus explained further the depth behind the commandments which were given centuries earlier:

> Do not think that I have come to abolish the Law or the Prophets; I have not come to abolish them but to fulfil them. I tell you the truth, until heaven and earth disappear, not the smallest letter, not the least stroke of a pen, will by any means disappear from the Law until everything is accomplished.

You have heard that it was said to the people long ago, 'Do not murder, and anyone who murders will be subject to judgment.' But I tell you that anyone who is angry with his brother without a cause, will be subject to judgment.

You have heard that it was said, 'Do not commit adultery.' But I tell you that anyone who looks at a woman lustfully has already committed adultery with her in his heart. If your right eye causes you to sin, gouge it out and throw it away. It is better for you to lose one part of your body than for your whole body to be thrown into hell. And if your right hand causes you to sin, cut it off and throw it away. It is better for you to lose one part of your body than for your whole body to go into hell.

It has been said, 'Anyone who divorces his wife must give her a certificate of divorce.' But I tell you that anyone who divorces his wife, except for marital unfaithfulness, causes her to become an adulteress, and anyone who marries the divorced woman commits adultery.

Again, you have heard that it was said to the people long ago, 'Do not break your oath, but keep the oaths you have made to the Lord.' But I tell you, Do not swear at all: either by heaven, for it is God's throne; or by the earth, for it is his footstool; or by Jerusalem, for it is the city of the Great King. And do not swear by your head, for you cannot make even one hair white or black. Simply let your 'Yes' be 'Yes,' and your 'No,' 'No'; anything beyond this comes from the evil one.

You have heard that it was said, 'Eye for eye, and tooth for tooth.' But I tell you, Do not resist an evil person. If someone strikes you on the right cheek, turn to him the other also. And if someone wants to sue you and take your tunic, let him have your cloak as well. If someone forces you to go one mile, go with him two miles. Give to the one who asks you, and do not turn away from the one who wants to borrow from you.

You have heard that it was said, 'Love your neighbour and hate your enemy.' But I tell you: Love your enemies and pray for those who persecute you, that you may be sons of your Father in heaven. He causes his sun to rise on the evil and the good, and sends rain on the righteous and the unrighteous. If you love those who love you, what reward will you get? Are not even the tax collectors doing that? And if you greet only your brothers, what are you doing more than others? Do not even pagans do that? Be perfect, therefore, as your heavenly Father is perfect.[3]

God hates sin

Clearly, God's standard is higher than we see in others, or in the mirror. If God is holy, then it is inevitable that sin will be abhorrent to Him. Thankfully, He has never been able to accommodate what is clearly alien from the purity and perfection which is His. For us, sin has become the norm. The tragedy is that though we were made in the image of God, we have, of our own volition, made ourselves sinful. We cannot imagine a world without corruption. It is easy to be flippant about it: the actress Mae West said, 'I used to be snow white, but I drifted.' But I think the French writer Alfred de Musset, was being more honest when he mused, 'I wore vice like a garment; now it is stuck to my skin.' When we stop to consider that God is good, it is straightforward to see that He hates our sins, which are the very opposite of who He is.

That is where the concept of 'repentance' comes in. We have seen cartoons of a monk carrying a placard with the words, 'Repent – the end is nigh'. Actually though, the word 'repent' gives great hope. God is not blind or blinkered when it comes to our sinful ways. He knows us better than we know ourselves. He weighs our thoughts, words, deeds and motives. But in contrast to the pioneers of most religions, God does not instruct us to try harder. Christianity is not about self-improvement. How could 'self', which is so flawed, help us? Like thorns on a bramble bush, however you grasp them, they hurt. Whichever way you look at people, it is evident 'that all have sinned, and fall short of the glory of God.' And sin that is not dealt with destroys us. God's remedy is that He commands all people everywhere to repent.

Repentance is turning to God from going our own way and ignoring Him. It is acknowledging that we are not the people we ought to be, but asking God to make all things new. A child who has a splinter in his or her finger doesn't need a plaster, or iodine, but for the offending splinter to be pulled out. Similarly, we need to turn from the wrong in our lives and look to God for forgiveness. C.S. Lewis said, 'Fallen man is not simply an imperfect creature who needs improvement; he is a rebel who must lay down his arms ... This process of surrender is what Christians call repentance. Now repentance is no fun at all. It is something much harder than eating humble pie. It means unlearning all the self-conceit and self-will that we have been training ourselves into for thousands of years. It means killing part of ourselves, undergoing a kind of death.'[4]

The Romans sometimes compelled a captive to be punished by tying them face to face with a dead body, then making them carry the corpse about until the horrible effluvia destroyed the life of the living victim. The classic writer Virgil described this horrid, cruel punishment:

> The living and the dead at his command
> >   were couple face to face, and hand to hand
> 'Til choked with stench, in hated embraces tied
> >   the lingering wretches pined away and died.

Every person needs to recognise that sin is deadly; it cuts us off from God, would keep us out of heaven, and condemn us to hell. God commands us to repent – to renounce it, and turn from it. He wants us to come clean, promising to forgive those who repent. We were born with our faces turned against God, repentance is turning around so that we are facing toward Him. An old American proverb says, 'If you want to clear the stream, get the hog out of the spring.' That is in essence what God does, when someone turns to Him for new life.

Charles Colson was involved in Watergate, the USA's worst political scandal. He once said he would 'walk over his own grandmother' to get Richard Nixon re-elected as president. He had been a Marine Commander and Special Counsel to the President of the USA, but his involvement in the Watergate affair led to his seven-month imprisonment. It was while awaiting trial that he was converted to Christ. An old friend had begun to read C.S. Lewis' book, 'Mere Christianity' with him. The biggest battle he faced in repenting was his 'spiritual cancer' of pride, yet he had an overwhelming sense that he was unclean. In his car, about to drive home, he broke down in floods of tears as he repented, confessed his sin to God, and asked for forgiveness. One biography says of him that repentance 'transferred his huge drive, intellect and maniacal energy from the service of Richard Nixon to the service of Jesus Christ.'[5]

God forgives sin

Christians are not people who have got it all together. They have no cause for smug self-righteousness. God has no time for the self-righteous. Self-satisfaction is far from being a Christian virtue. Christians cannot boast about their acceptance by God, for they have done nothing – and *cannot* do anything – to earn it. They have simply received what Jesus has purchased for them. They are forgiven sinners. Their righteousness has been given to them in exchange for all their wrong. There is a revealing passage in the New Testament giving us insight into the members of the church in the city of Corinth. They were certainly not 'do-gooders' – notice especially the hinge in the passage, which has the words, 'And such were some of you'. Clearly, the church comprised people who had failed but found new life in Jesus:

> Do you not know that the wicked will not inherit the kingdom of God? Do not be deceived: Neither the sexually immoral nor idolaters nor adulterers nor male prostitutes nor homosexual offenders nor thieves nor the greedy nor drunkards nor slanderers nor swindlers will inherit the kingdom of God. And that is what some of you were. But you were washed, you were sanctified, you were justified in the name of the Lord Jesus Christ and by the Spirit of our God.[6]

The apostle Paul underlined this truth when referring to himself as 'the chief of sinners'. He wrote, 'For it is by grace you have been saved, through faith – and this not from yourselves, it is the gift of God – not of works, so that no-one can boast.'[7] In other words, Christian experience, righteousness and heaven itself are not rewards, but gifts from God to all who will receive them.

ENDNOTES

1 James 1:17 & 4:1&2
2 Matthew 22:37-38, NKJV
3 Matthew 5:17-18, 21-22, 27-48
4 C.S.Lewis *Mere Christianity*, Fount Publishing, 1977
5 Jonathan Aitken *Charles Colson: A Life Redeemed*, Continuum, 2006
6 1 Corinthians 6:9-11
7 Ephesians 2:8 & 9

FOUR

A Christian has received what Jesus offers

Jesus is different

Jesus stands out as the towering figure of history. Millions today from all nations across the world and from all cultures follow Him because, having discovered who He is and what He did, they find Him altogether worthy of their trust, worship and service.

No one ever spoke as Jesus did. And all that He said was perfectly consistent with all He had been living. The Sermon on the Mount was really Jesus' biography. That famous message was merely translating His life into words. There was no hypocrisy in the life of Jesus. He went about only doing good. He was engaged in prayer and fervent activity. He was sociable, but often retreated to be alone with His Father. He was tempted in every way as we are, yet He never sinned. He did not have material possessions, even contrasting Himself to foxes and birds, which have their holes and birds their nests, but He, the Son of Man, having nowhere to lay His head. Though meek and gentle, He was outspoken in His exposure of religious hypocrisy and so was hated by many of the leaders of His day. Yet the ordinary people gladly listened to Him. He cared for the underdogs, the waifs and strays of society. Children loved to be in His presence.

Jesus is one with God

As Jesus walked along the roads of Galilee, often alone, His thoughts were at one with His Father. In times of rest, during the journeys by boat that He made or with His disciples after a day's exhausting preaching, His thoughts were taken up with His heavenly Father. When He was alone, without His disciples, and among the hills where He liked to go, He was consumed with God. And when busy teaching, healing, meeting the needs of those He met, His constant object of thought was His Father. This was the natural orientation of His heart, mind and soul, the 'food' that constantly nourished Him. He would say that He delighted to do His Father's will, and delighted to fulfil the law of God. He was at one in thought, word and activity with His Father.

Swiss historian Philip Schaff (1819-1893) said of Jesus:

> Jesus of Nazareth, without money and arms, conquered more millions than Alexander, Caesar, Mohammed and Napoleon; without science and learning He shed more light on things human and divine than all the philosophers and scholars combined; without the eloquence of the school, He spoke words of life such as were never spoken before nor since and produced effects that lie beyond the reach of orator or poet; without writing a single line, He has set more pens in motion and furnished themes for more sermons, orations, discussions, works of art, learned volumes, and sweet songs of praise than the whole army of great men of ancient and modern times.

Jesus' death is central

And yet, it is the death of Jesus that is central to the faith of Christians. The cross, which of course was the place of execution, has become the emblem of Christianity. Throughout His ministry, Jesus repeatedly spoke of His impending death, burial and resurrection. After the four Gospels describing Jesus' life from birth to ascension, the New Testament is saturated with His cross and resurrection. It is the theme of the message proclaimed throughout the world and described in the Book of Acts. It dominates the Letters written by Paul, Peter, John and others, and it is uppermost in the songs of heaven which are recorded in the Book of Revelation, the last book of the Bible.

But then the cross was anticipated throughout the years of the Old Testament, as the prophets spoke in detail about how the coming Messiah would suffer and what would be accomplished through His death. Jewish religious rituals, which included the sacrifice of animals as a payment for sin, were each pre-figuring Jesus 'the Lamb of God' who would take away the sin of the world. The characters of the Old Testament 'saw Jesus' by faith as they looked forward to Jesus' death for sin, just as we look back 2,000 years to His sacrifice.

Jesus was given a series of false trials, which were a travesty of the Roman judicial system. He was mocked and railed against. Soldiers smote, spat upon and scourged Jesus. He was stripped of His garments, and mercilessly flogged with a whip, in which were embedded fragments of bone. They plucked out His beard, and wedged on His sensitive brow a crown of thorns, which pierced His skin. On that raw back He was compelled to carry a rough, rugged, Roman cross. Nails were hammered through His hands and feet, as He was hung naked between two crucified thieves, and between heaven and earth on that cross.

Behind His crucifixion was a cowardly politician, and a fickle crowd led by jealous religious leaders and known agitators. The Roman soldiers would have made vulgar jokes, taunted Him with filthy talk as they poured their vitriol on Jesus. Yet, in every way Jesus had been altogether lovely in His dealings with the people, whom He had gone out of His way to meet. He had loved people so much but was subjected to despicable, humiliating and barbarous treatment, normally reserved by the Romans for those who commit the most heinous crimes.

Jesus could have called legions of angels to rescue Him. He could have cursed those who were crucifying Him. Yet, He prayed for their forgiveness, and gave Himself over to death out of love for everyone who has shaken his or her fist in the face of God. He died for all of us who have, in effect, said 'We don't want you to rule over us.' The reason Jesus had to die in this way, which was so utterly shameful by human standards, lies in God's plan for rescuing sinful humanity.

This was not a tragic accident like Princess Diana being killed in a crushed car in a Paris underpass in the early hours of a Sunday morning. Jesus, the King of kings, the One whom before whom every knee will bow, deliberately gave Himself to humiliation, shame, suffering and death on a cross.

Jesus' death was for our sin

Hanging and bleeding on the cross, Jesus took on Himself the anger of God against sin. The triune God has an uncompromising, unrelenting hatred of sin. For humanity to be saved from eternal condemnation, our sin had to be paid for. God's plan of love was that the Father sent the Son to be the Saviour of the world.

Jesus took the heat of God's wrath as He carried our sin on Himself. Nails did not keep Jesus on the cross, but rather His love for His Father and for you and me. John, the youngest of Jesus' twelve disciples, witnessed the crucifixion and later wrote, 'Here is love, not that we loved God, but that He loved us and sent His Son to be the propitiation for our sins.'[1] 'Propitiation' is the substitute carrying the full weight of God's rightful anger against sin and guilt.

Jesus was dying to buy us back into the relationship with God which we were created to enjoy. We are cut off from God, and in a sorry state, because of our sin, but Jesus paid a sufficient price with His own blood, to redeem us. The Bible says of Jesus, 'In whom we have redemption through His blood.'[2] The natural reaction to being bought, not with corruptible things like silver and gold, but with the precious blood of Jesus, is that we will want to live for Him. Sadly, because a ransom has been paid, it does not necessarily mean we will inevitably respect and follow the redeemer. Famously, John Paul Getty III was kidnapped, his ear severed and then he was held for a ransom. His grandfather paid millions of dollars for his release. But young Getty became an alcoholic and drug addict, which led to liver failure, and a stroke, which left him a quadriplegic and nearly blind, then prematurely dead. It was hardly what his grandfather would have wanted for a grandson for whom he had paid so dearly. Similarly, it is too easy to squander the love of Jesus by turning our back on Him and going our own way.

If you have ever visited a law court, you will have experienced the heightened sense of tension before the verdict is given. So, the big issue for each of us is what we will do with Jesus? Because He has paid for sin, we can be acquitted and declared 'just' in the sight of God. Jesus carried all our sins on the cross 2,000 years ago, but the moment we trust Him, His righteousness is transferred to us, so that in the sight of God we are covered in the goodness of Jesus. We have a new standing before God. This is illustrated in a parable Jesus told, that we find in Luke 18:

> To some who were confident of their own righteousness and looked down on everybody else, Jesus told this parable: 'Two men went up to the temple to pray, one a Pharisee and the other a tax collector. The Pharisee stood up and prayed about himself: "God, I thank you that I am not like other men – robbers, evildoers, adulterers – or even like this tax collector. I fast twice a week and give a tenth of all I get."
>
> 'But the tax collector stood at a distance. He would not even look up to heaven, but beat his breast and said, "God, have mercy on me, a sinner."
>
> I tell you that this man, rather than the other, went home justified before *God*.'

The French mathematician and philosopher, Blaise Pascal reflecting on this parable wrote, 'There are two kinds of men: the righteous who think they are sinners, and the sinners who think they are righteous.'

Jesus' death brings us to God

The catalyst for the Reformation which spread through Europe 500 years ago was the great re-discovery of the doctrine of 'justification by faith.' It means that we can be declared 'just' simply by putting our trust in Jesus. It is not what we do that brings us to God, it is what Jesus has done. Martin Luther, the great German reformer, wrote this to a monk who was distressed, because he had no assurance that his sin was forgiven or that he was accepted by God,

> Learn to know Christ and Him crucified. Learn to sing to Him and say, "Lord Jesus, you are my righteousness; I am your sin. You took on you what was mine, yet set on me what was yours. You became what you were not, that I might become what I was not."

That is exactly what makes a person a Christian.

We picture Jesus on the cross with His arms outstretched. It is as if they are reaching to lost humanity, to bring us to God. We who have been God's enemies can experience reconciliation, and enter into a new relationship with God and His people. The Bible says, 'For when we were God's enemies, we were reconciled to him by the death of his Son.'[3]

Having taken our sin on Himself, Jesus gave Himself over to death. He cried out, 'It is finished.' Then He prayed, 'Father, into your hands I commit my spirit', and He died. Some of His followers gained permission to take down the body of Jesus from the cross. They wrapped it tightly with spices in cloths and laid it in a previously unused tomb. The grave was sealed with a huge millstone and guarded. For three days His dead, cold body lay there until the first Easter Sunday morning. Then the stone was rolled away, not so much to let out Jesus, but to let Jesus' followers look in and see the tomb empty with the cloths lying as if there was still a body in them.

Over the next forty days Jesus, with nail prints still in His hands, feet and the spear wound in His side, appeared to over 520 people, convincing even the doubters of His resurrection. The best news that the world ever had came from a tomb cut in a rock face. The only biography of anyone that does not end with death and burial is Jesus'. He did something no religious or political leader could ever do, because He is the God-man. The resurrection is God's acceptance of Jesus' sacrifice for sin. A new era has dawned, and we can enter into the joy of it.

Jesus has conquered death

The same power that raised Jesus from the dead is operative within the lives of those who trust Him as their Lord and Saviour. C.S. Lewis said, 'Jesus has forced open a door that had been locked since the death of the first man. He has met, fought and beaten the King of Death. Everything is different because He has done so.'

Before a person is converted, there is usually a growing, if secret, desire to know God. This is often the beginning of faith. The Bible explains this as the work of God the Holy Spirit in the life and thoughts of a person. And Jesus promised that those who search for Him will find Him.

God merely spoke words to bring all of creation into being, but to bring us into a relationship with Himself cost the crucifixion of His Son. Clearly, our 'salvation' (as the Bible calls it) is of the utmost importance to God.

Many hope that trying to be good will please their god. The Christian recognises that he or she can never be good enough to be at ease in the presence of a totally good God. We are convinced that God does not love us because of any goodness in us, but that God can make us His, simply because He does love us. God takes the initiative. He calls us to Himself. It is He who forgives a person and begins the work of transforming that person to become increasingly like Jesus.

The actor Cary Grant was met in the street by an excited man, who stopped him and said, 'Wait a minute, I know who you are – don't tell me – err … Rock Hudson … no … you're ….' Cary Grant thought he would help and said, 'I'm Cary Grant.' The man replied, 'No that's not it ... you're ...!' There comes a moment when we need to simply believe Jesus for who He is, and for what He has done. Faith, even if it appears very weak, gives us access to God. The Bible teaches that whoever believes, or trusts in Jesus will be saved.

Christian conversion involves a 'death' to our self – we accept that we have got things wrong and need God to save us. Then there is a new, spiritual birth whereby we are given life from heaven itself. It is the life of God within the innermost being of men and women. It is the start of a life lived with God, through the good as well as the tough times, and on into eternity.

ENDNOTES

1   1 John 4:10, NKJV.
2   Colossians 1:14, NKJV.
3   Romans 5:10

Five

A Christian is revelling in what they have

Most of us perceive ourselves to be missing something; we often feel incomplete, empty yet cluttered and longing for something or someone beyond ourselves. We recognise that we are not alone in these questionings. Louise Fletcher Tarkington was a well known 20th century American novelist. She led a hard life, being married to an alcoholic playwright who she eventually divorced. Their only daughter was schizophrenic and died of pneumonia aged just 16. Louise died a year later. She is best remembered for her poem 'Beginning again'. The first verse expresses what many feel, even if they have not been through all that she endured:

> I wish there were some wonderful place
> > In the Land of Beginning Again
> Where all our mistakes and all our heartaches
> > And all of our poor selfish grief
> Could be dropped like a shabby old coat at the door
> > And never put on again.

When we are trying to deal with a number of difficulties, which seem to come in clusters, thoughts of 'religion' merely aggravate an already irritating quest. But, knowing and trusting Jesus is not 'religion' as we usually understand it. Jesus gives to us the reality of knowing the living Creator walking with us and living within us, so that life without Him appears meaningless. This happens not by imbibing religion but by receiving Jesus into our lives as our individual Lord and Saviour. Jesus said, 'I tell you the truth, unless you are converted and become like children, you will never enter the kingdom of heaven.'[1]

Jesus changes lives

The world's most memorable Christian conversion is that of Saul of Tarsus. This devout, strict Jewish leader and academic bitterly opposed the early followers of Jesus. One amazing day, travelling from Jerusalem to Damascus to persecute Christians in that city, he was dramatically confronted by the risen Jesus, with the words, 'Saul, Saul, why do you persecute me?' It led to a complete turnaround, so that for the next three decades Saul, whose name was changed to Paul, gave himself to proclaiming the good news of 'Jesus Christ and Him crucified.' Not all conversions are so dramatic, but each involves an individual turning from sin, and to Jesus, only to find that actually He has turned to them.

Once that happens, the new Christian finds that different desires and priorities, as well as a fresh power, take over their lives. Responding to God in this way means that the person begins to live with a consciousness of His presence with them 24/7. There is a growing confidence about the meaning of even the most inconsequential things of life. God becomes the beginning and end of everything; the be-all and end-all of life. That does not lead to monasticism or isolation but to a new involvement in society, life and work. There is a recognition that our world is really God's, and that He has the right to rule. The author of the Christmas carol, 'O little town of Bethlehem', Phillips Brooks expressed this well, 'When God says to your disturbed, distracted, restless soul or mind, "Come unto Me," He is saying, come out of the strife and doubt and struggle of what is at the moment where you stand, into that which was and is and is to be – the eternal, the essential, the absolute.'

Jesus changes our future

There is so much for which to be grateful, which leads to an attitude of gratitude, even contentment. The believer's name is, in Biblical language, 'written in the

Lamb's Book of Life.' In other words, Christians have the certainty that heaven is their eternal home. Most cities are open to all, but heaven is not like that. The Bible says of it, 'The glory and honour of the nations will be brought into it. Nothing impure will ever enter it, nor will anyone who does what is shameful or deceitful, but only those whose names are written in the Lamb's book of life.'[2] But the sin which should lead to condemnation and exclusion from heaven, has been forgiven. There is no condemnation for those who have trusted Jesus. Blaise Pascal (1623–1662) mused that 'it is not certain that everything is uncertain!' The Christian rests on God's promises in the Bible and has a quiet, non-presumptuous assurance that all is well with their soul for all eternity.

Of course, one day each of us will die; undertakers are never out of work! Death for the Christian is but the doorway to eternal life. At the moment of death, the Christian is taken to be with the Lord forever. Eventually, on the resurrection day, God will re-form our bodies, which will be united again to our souls. I feel sure that these resurrection bodies will be recognisable, even if different from the bodies we now have. Does this seem fanciful? Well, read on!

Jesus changes our past

Michael Faraday (1791–1867), the great English chemist and physicist, discovered the principle of electromagnetic induction which is the basis for the electric generator and motor. He was a devout Christian. One day a workman who was helping Faraday knocked a little silver cup into a jar of strong acid. The cup was almost immediately dissolved. Faraday put some chemicals into the jar, and quickly the silver which had disintegrated settled to the bottom. Faraday retrieved this shapeless mass of silver and sent it to a silversmith. It was restored shining, beautiful and bright as before. If Faraday and a silversmith could do that to the destroyed silver cup, I have no difficulty believing that God will one day give us resurrection bodies from the dust or ashes of the ground in which we have been laid.

Christians are sure of this because they know that their sins have been blotted out. They have experienced forgiveness and pardon. The Bible has many ways to portray this: sins separated from us as far as the east is from the west; sins cast behind God's back; sins washed away; sins and iniquities remembered no more; sins cast into the deepest ocean, but each underlines the great truth that because of Jesus' finished work, we can know complete cleansing from our past and our future sins. If forgiveness depended upon what we could achieve, or that somehow we had to do sufficient good to outweigh our bad, there could never be certainty. We would always live with the fear that we haven't been good enough or accomplished sufficient to pacify or even please God, and consequently that our future beyond death is highly questionable. The future would create only fear. But forgiveness is a gift, and the future is something to which Christians eagerly look forward. Earlier, we cut short a famous Bible verse, but it continues: 'The wages of sin is death, but the gift of God is eternal life in Christ Jesus our Lord.'[3]

Sir Wilfred Grenfell was a missionary doctor in Labrador. He recalls, though, an earlier experience as a young hospital doctor in the U.K. A woman with terrible burns was brought in. He saw immediately that there was no hope for her. Apparently, her husband had come home drunk and thrown a paraffin lamp over her. The police were called, but they brought to the hospital a magistrate and the now half-sobered husband. The magistrate leaned over the bed insisting that the patient tell the police exactly what happened. She turned from side to side, avoiding looking at her husband who stood at the foot of the bed.

Finally, her eyes came to rest on his hands and, slowly, on his face. The look of suffering disappeared from her face and in its place there came one of tenderness, love and all the beautiful things that a woman's face can express. She looked back then to the magistrate and said in a quiet, clear voice: 'Sir, it was just an accident.' Grenfell said, 'With a shadow of a smile still on her face, she snuggled down in the pillows and died.' Then he added, 'That was like God, and God is like that. His love sees through our sins.' However, Jesus did not deny or overlook our sin, but freely, lovingly carried it on Himself.

Jesus changes our present

At conversion, God by His Holy Spirit, comes to live
in the heart, mind and life of the Christian. The new
believer becomes a 'child' of the living God. He or she
is adopted into His family, and given adult standing in
His family. 'We receive the Spirit of adoption whereby
we cry "Abba, Father"' The Holy Spirit is God Himself,
powerfully at work in the world today, and living within
all who have looked to God for salvation. God does not
move people as we would move stones, but He puts life
– His life – into them. The Spirit of God gives us new
desires[4], so that 'if anyone is in Christ, he/she is a new
creation; old things have passed away; behold, all things
have become new.'[5] It means that we can go through life
knowing that God is with us; we have a new freedom
which entails having within us the power to do what
God would want us to; we want to speak up for Jesus,
even to a generation that appears as though it doesn't
want to hear the voice of God. Though there is a great
inheritance waiting for us, those who follow Jesus are
by no means immune to suffering. Yet Christians find
that God never wastes any tears or pain, time or toil.

The Bible, God's Word, becomes a delight, as God
'speaks' to them, and Christians find that prayer ceases
to be an emergency rip cord in times of trouble, but
like breathing, is natural and spontaneous, a delightful
discipline, which brings them to the very heart of
heaven. And church - the place where God's people
meet to worship, work and witness – is something

Christians love. Church becomes the highlight of the week. Hungering and thirsting after God increasingly grows to become the passion of their lives because He has come to mean everything to them.

Jesus can change YOU!

Is this your experience? Have you been converted to Christ? Have you trusted Jesus as your Lord and Saviour? Are you following Him? Would you be willing to pray now and commit yourself to Him? In an act of repentance and faith, would you call on the name of the Lord Jesus and be saved? If so, please pray something like this now:

> Dear God, my Heavenly Father, Thank you that you know everything there is to know about me. I want to say that I am sorry for my sin, and with your help I want to turn from it. I do believe that Jesus came to earth and died for me: He rose from the dead. Please forgive me. Become my Lord, my Saviour and constant Companion. By your Holy Spirit, come and live within me and help me to follow you. Thank you for hearing this prayer, which I pray in Jesus' name. Amen.

If you genuinely pray this prayer, God will hear and answer. Prolific Christian writer Warren Wiersbe, says, 'When you are sick, you want a doctor not a medical book or formula. When you are being sued, you want a lawyer and not a law book. Likewise, when you face your last enemy, death, you want a Saviour and not a doctrine written in a book. In Jesus Christ every doctrine is made personal. When you belong to Him, you have all you will ever need in life, death, time and eternity.'[6]

I would love to hear from you, and send you some further reading to help you move forward in your Christian faith. As you follow Jesus, you will find increasing joy, and the blessing of Him moulding and making you the person you were created to be.

ENDNOTES

1 Matthew 18:3, NASB
2 Revelation 21:26-27
3 Romans 6:23
4 See Romans 8:14-17
5 2 Corinthians 5:17, NKJV
6 Warren Wiersbe, *The Bible Exposition Commentary Vol 1*, Chariot Victor Publishing, 2003

*Other Books available
from
Christian Focus Publications.*

ISBN 978-1-84550-242-3

Things God Wants Us to Know
Find Purpose in your life

ROGER CARSWELL

Everybody has an opinion about God - but few people actually are brave enough to think it through. Thinking about God may result in changing things about your life! Many are prepared to share what they think about God but not so many have ever asked 'What does God want us to know about Him?' Here is just such a guide that distills the essence of the Christian message to those prepared to look for God.

Roger Carswell has spent many years explaining the Christian message to people, that experience comes through in this gift book that gently opens up a world of opportunities to those prepared to start thinking. Do you love someone enough to share the gospel with them? *Things God Wants Us to Know* will enable you to do this so that they can read it reflectively in their own time.

> ... it is a lucid presentation of the gospel full of contemporary allusions, vivid illustrations and packs a powerful gospel punch. Open-minded friends would be pleased to be given this solid little book.
>
> John Benton
> Managing Editor, *Evangelicals Now*

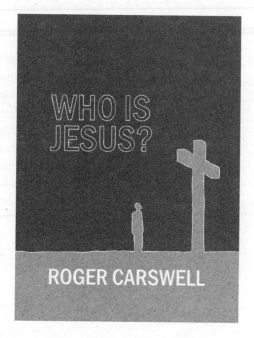

ISBN 978-1-84550-635-3

Who is Jesus?

ROGER CARSWELL

What do a teenager, an American journalist and a German reformer all have in common? Like so many others they have heard the original, authoritative and godly words of Jesus and in this book you will find out how. Roger Carswell was the teenager who was introduced to Jesus by his uncle after a game of tennis. Let Roger introduce you to this same Jesus so that you can meet Him for yourself and find out who He is and what He has done for you. Take a moment to understand who is the real, historical Jesus and why knowing Him matters to you today.

Christian Focus Publications

Our mission statement –

STAYING FAITHFUL
In dependence upon God we seek to impact the world through literature faithful to His infallible Word, the Bible. Our aim is to ensure that the Lord Jesus Christ is presented as the only hope to obtain forgiveness of sin, live a useful life and look forward to heaven with Him.

Our Books are published in four imprints:

CHRISTIAN
FOCUS

Popular works including biographies, commentaries, basic doctrine and Christian living.

CHRISTIAN
HERITAGE

Books representing some of the best material from the rich heritage of the church.

MENTOR

Books written at a level suitable for Bible College and seminary students, pastors, and other serious readers. The imprint includes commentaries, doctrinal studies, examination of current issues and church history.

CF4•K

Children's books for quality Bible teaching and for all age groups: Sunday school curriculum, puzzle and activity books; personal and family devotional titles, biographies and inspirational stories – Because you are never too young to know Jesus!

Christian Focus Publications Ltd,
Geanies House, Fearn, Ross-shire,
IV20 1TW, Scotland, United Kingdom.
www.christianfocus.com